WHAT DO YOU KNOW ABOUT

Child abuse

PETE SANDERS and STEVE MYERS

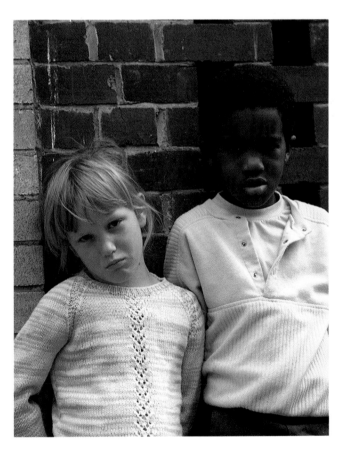

W

FRANKLIN WATTS
LONDON • SYDNEY

This edition published in 2000
© Aladdin Books Ltd 1995

Designed and produced by
Aladdin Books Ltd
28 Percy Street
London W1P 0LD

First published in Great Britain in
1995 by Franklin Watts
96 Leonard Street
London EC2A 4XD

ISBN: 0 7496 2096 X (hardback)
ISBN: 0 7496 3817 6 (paperback)

A catalogue record for this book is
available from the British Library

Printed in Belgium

Design   David West
                Children's Book
                Design
Editor   Sarah Levete
Picture research Brooks Krikler
                Research
Illustrator   Mike Lacey

Pete Sanders is Senior Lecturer in health education at the University of North London. He was a head teacher for ten years and has written many books on social issues for children.

Steve Myers is a freelance writer. He has co-written other titles in this series and has worked on several educational projects for children.

The consultant, Dr Judith Trowell, is a child and adolescent psychiatrist at the Tavistock Clinic.

CONTENTS

HOW TO USE THIS BOOK

The books in this series are intended to help young people to understand more about the issues that may affect their lives.

At the end of the book there is a section called "What Can We Do?" This presents suggestions and ideas, helping the reader to develop a sense of citizenship. Organisations and helplines are also listed, to provide additional sources of information and support.

Each book can be read by a child alone, or together with a parent, carer, teacher or helper. Issues raised in the storyline are further discussed in the accompanying text, so that there is an opportunity to talk through ideas as they come up.

INTRODUCTION

MOST PEOPLE WOULD NEVER DREAM OF CAUSING DELIBERATE HARM OR UNHAPPINESS TO A CHILD OR YOUNG PERSON.

Unfortunately, many children and young people live in situations where they are subjected to abuse.

This book explains what child abuse is, and the different forms it can take. Each chapter introduces a different aspect of the subject, illustrated by a continuing storyline. The characters in the story have to deal with situations which many people may face at some point in their lives.

After each episode, we stop and look at the issues raised, and widen out the discussion. By the end, you will know more about child abuse, why some people become abusers and the effect that abuse can have both on sufferers and those close to them.

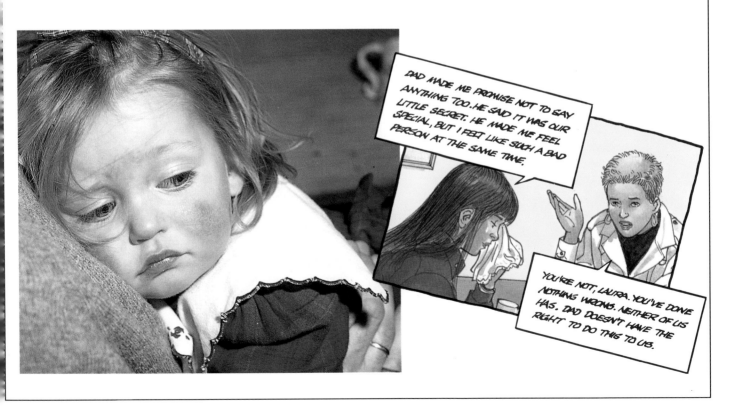

DAD MADE ME PROMISE NOT TO SAY ANYTHING TOO. HE SAID IT WAS OUR LITTLE SECRET. HE MADE ME FEEL SPECIAL, BUT I FELT LIKE SUCH A BAD PERSON AT THE SAME TIME.

YOU'RE NOT, LAURA. YOU'VE DONE NOTHING WRONG. NEITHER OF US HAS. DAD DOESN'T HAVE THE RIGHT TO DO THIS TO US.

WHAT IS CHILD ABUSE?

EVERY YOUNG PERSON HAS THE RIGHT TO GROW UP WITHOUT BEING HARMED BY OTHERS, AND TO HAVE HIS OR HER BASIC NEEDS MET.

However, there are people who choose to ignore the rights and feelings of children.

To abuse someone means to mistreat or harm that person deliberately, either physically or mentally. Everyone gets hurt now and again, and this may sometimes be as a result of the action of somebody else. But being hurt by accident is very different from being deliberately abused.

There are four different kinds of abuse. These are physical, emotional and sexual abuse, and neglect. Sometimes young people are subjected to more than one kind of abuse at the same time. It may happen just once, or it may go on for a long time – perhaps for many years. Some people believe that certain forms of abuse are more serious than others. However, it is important to remember that all forms of abuse are wrong and that they are never the fault of the person who is being abused.

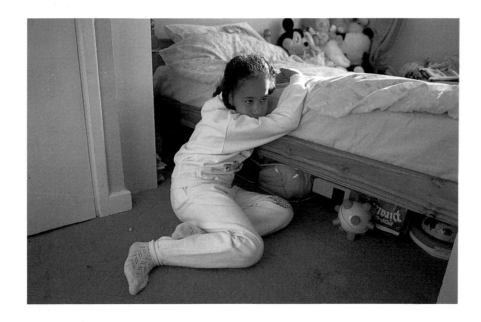

Every child and young person has the right to be protected and loved. No form of abuse is acceptable.

▽ Laura Swann and her friends had gone to the park to play after school one evening.

▽ Fatima and Stuart went over to Laura.

◁ Laura was upset. Before the others could stop her, she ran off into the park.

◁ They searched for Laura for a while. There was no sign of her. They decided she had made her own way home.

▽ When Laura arrived at school the next day, her friends were waiting for her.

▽ Tim came across and apologised to Laura.

Fatima is worried about being late.
Each family is unique. Not all parents and carers have the same ideas about raising children and discipline. Some believe in being strict; others might be more easy-going. They may be influenced by particular cultural or religious beliefs. Most parents' and carers' attitudes to discipline are formed because of their concern for the well-being and safety of their children.

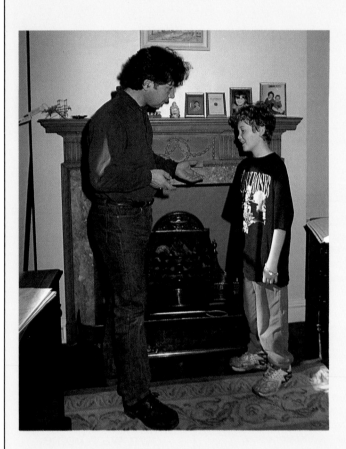

Laura has run off to the woods alone.
Child abusers may take advantage of isolated and dark places so it is important to be sensible about where you go. Always use well-lit paths and if possible walk with a group. Although most abuse is carried out by people known to the child, never accept a lift from or go off with a stranger, even if he or she knows your name or claims to be a friend of someone you know.

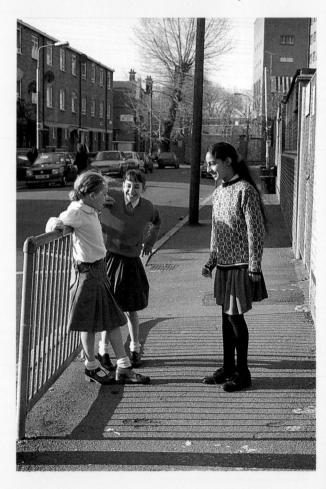

Many parents and carers have rules which they expect children to follow.
These can seem unfair, particularly if you feel you should be allowed more freedom to decide for yourself.

One common rule involves being home by a certain time. Usually this is because parents and carers want to be sure that their children are safe. If you are going to be late, phoning home can save a lot of worry, and is a responsible and adult thing to do.

PHYSICAL ABUSE AND NEGLECT

PHYSICAL ABUSE IS AN ACTION WHICH INTENTIONALLY CAUSES HARM TO A YOUNG PERSON'S BODY. NEGLECT IS THE FAILURE OF PARENTS OR CARERS TO MEET A YOUNG PERSON'S BASIC PHYSICAL AND EMOTIONAL NEEDS.

Physical abuse may take the form of hitting, kicking, punching, biting, scratching, shaking violently or even burning. It can also mean giving a child dangerous drugs or poisons.

Young people have suffered terrible and even fatal injuries as a result of physical abuse. Their bones may have been broken, or they may have been burned with cigarettes. Not all abuse is this severe. Some children are physically abused for years without their injuries needing special treatment, although they might frequently have cuts and bruises which they try to explain away.

Neglect can mean that a young person is not given enough food, is kept in the cold or dark, or is left alone for a long time. It could be that parents do not obtain medical help when the child needs it.

Neglect is being deprived of the things which are essential to our physical and emotional well-being. It does not mean being denied everything we want! In extreme cases of neglect, children have starved to death because they have not been fed, even though the parents or carers themselves may have eaten well. Or the children may have been left to look after themselves.

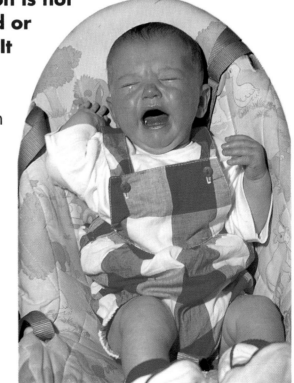

Some children have been left for hours, or even days, without the care they need.

▽ A month later, Laura and her friends arranged to go to the cinema.

TIM SHOULD BE HERE BY NOW. HE'S BEEN TALKING ABOUT SEEING THIS FILM FOR WEEKS, AND IT STARTS IN AN HOUR.

I'VE GOT MY BIKE WITH ME. I COULD RIDE ROUND TO HIS HOUSE AND SEE WHAT'S KEEPING HIM.

I'LL COME WITH YOU. YOU KNOW WHAT HIS DAD'S LIKE.

▽ Tim answered the door. He'd been crying. He said he couldn't come out.

WHAT'S THE MATTER? WE THOUGHT YOU WERE GOING TO THE PICTURES WITH US.

IS IT YOUR DAD AGAIN? WHAT'S HAPPENED THIS TIME? HAS HE HIT YOU?

I FORGOT TO GET HIS PAPER LAST NIGHT. PLEASE GO AWAY. I CAN'T TALK NOW. YOU'LL ONLY MAKE THINGS WORSE.

▽ Suddenly, Tim's father appeared at the door.

WHAT ARE YOU TWO HANGING AROUND FOR? DIDN'T YOU HEAR HIM? CLEAR OFF!

COME ON, LAURA, WE'D BETTER GO. SEE YOU ON MONDAY, TIM.

▽ Tim was not at school on Monday. By Wednesday, his friends were worried about him.

I WISH WE COULD DO SOMETHING TO HELP. EVERYONE KNOWS WHAT HIS DAD'S LIKE WHEN HE'S HAD A DRINK.

WHAT CAN WE DO? STUART WENT ROUND THERE LAST NIGHT. TIM'S MUM SAID HE'S ILL. MAYBE HE IS. WE DON'T KNOW FOR SURE THAT HIS DAD HIT HIM.

WE MIGHT MAKE THINGS WORSE IF WE SAY ANYTHING. I'D BETTER BE GOING. MUM AND DAD ARE BOTH ON LATE SHIFTS, SO I'VE GOT TO PICK UP LUKE.

▽ Laura collected her brother from school and took him home. There was a letter from their sister, Maggie, in the mail.

LAURA, HURRY UP. I'M HUNGRY.

IN A MINUTE. I'M READING. MAGGIE'S ENJOYING BEING AT UNIVERSITY. SHE SOUNDS HAPPIER THAN SHE WAS AT HOME.

LATER THAT EVENING...

HOW'S MY LITTLE PRINCESS TONIGHT? YOU SMELL WONDERFUL.

YOU MADE ME JUMP! I HAD A BATH AND USED SOME OF MUM'S TALC. YOU SEEM IN A GOOD MOOD TONIGHT.

△ Laura was surprised. Her dad wasn't usually so affectionate.

Laura and her friends know that Tim's father beats him.

They believe that they cannot do anything about it because they are not adults, and that to become involved would only make things worse. It can be difficult to know what to do for the best in this situation. But if you do suspect that another young person is being abused, it is important to talk to an adult whom you trust. He or she may be able to do something about what is going on.

Some people believe that smacking is an effective form of punishment.

Usually a smack is meant as a reminder that the child has done something wrong, and is a warning not to do it again. But some people disagree with any form of physical punishment. Others say it is not harmful, saying it does not do any lasting damage to the child.

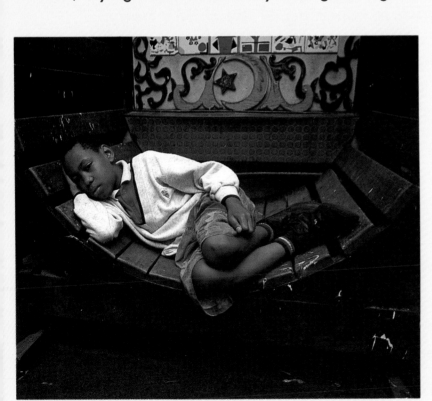

Laura is experiencing some neglect.

She is still young, but because her parents have to work long hours, Laura has to collect her brother from school, let herself into the house and make tea for them both. Although it is illegal in some countries for children below a certain age to be left alone in the house, many young people are in the same situation as Laura. Sometimes this is because there are financial pressures on the parents.

EMOTIONAL AND SEXUAL ABUSE

EMOTIONAL ABUSE MEANS UNDERMINING A YOUNG PERSON'S SELF CONFIDENCE AND EMOTIONAL WELL-BEING. SEXUAL ABUSE MEANS TAKING ADVANTAGE OF A YOUNG PERSON IN A SEXUAL MANNER.

Emotional abuse can involve continually ignoring a child, not showing any love or affection, or constantly ridiculing him or her. Children who are emotionally abused are often told that they are not loveable. They will not be praised or offered any encouragement. To the child, the abuser will often seem to be two different people – nice one minute and nasty the next. This can be very confusing for the young person.

Sexual abuse can mean forcing a young person to take part in sex acts. Or it may be inappropriate touching of the child's body. Sexual abuse imposes adult experiences on a child before he or she is physically or emotionally ready for them. An abuser might ask children to touch parts of his or her body, or show them rude pictures or videos. The behaviour of the abuser may at first appear innocent, and the young person might not realise what is happening.

Emotional abuse may involve a young person being criticised, taunted or humiliated, sometimes in front of other people.

▽ A few days later, Laura's mum was getting ready to go to work.

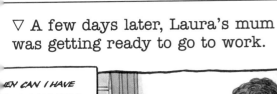

[EN] CAN I HAVE [N]EW TRAINERS, [M]UM? PAT'S GOT [M]E, AND YOU [P]ROMISED I COULD [H]AVE A PAIR TOO.

LAURA, I'M DOING MY BEST. I DON'T THINK YOU UNDERSTAND HOW MUCH THINGS COST, SOMETIMES.

DO YOU HAVE TO WORK LATE AGAIN, MUM?

YOU KNOW I DO, DARLING. NOW LAURA, YOUR DAD SHOULD BE BACK BY NINE O'CLOCK. MAKE SURE LUKE'S IN BED BY THE TIME HE GETS HOME.

I ALWAYS DO, DON'T I?

▽ When her dad arrived home, Laura told him about the trainers, and what her mum had said.

▷ Mrs Swann left. Laura felt really miserable.

[IT'] S NOT FAIR. MUM PROMISED [I'D] HAVE NEW TRAINERS NEXT [W]EEK. NOW WHAT AM I GOING [T]O DO?

DON'T WORRY, PRINCESS. I'LL SEE WHAT I CAN DO. HAVE I EVER LET YOU DOWN YET?

▽ Laura smiled. Her dad went upstairs for a bath.

DO ME A FAVOUR, PRINCESS, AND BRING ME UP THE PAPER, WOULD YOU?

OK, I'LL BE UP IN A MINUTE.

▽ By the time Laura went upstairs, her dad was already in the bath.

THANKS, PRINCESS. WHY DON'T [Y]OU COME IN AND TALK TO ME [F]OR A WHILE?

NOT WHEN YOU'RE IN THE BATH, DAD!

▽ The telephone rang. Relieved, Laura ran to answer it. It was Tim.

ARE YOU OK? WHEN YOU DIDN'T TURN UP FOR SCHOOL, WE WERE ALL REALLY WORRIED. TIM, HAS YOUR DAD BEEN HAVING A GO AT YOU?

YOU DON'T UNDERSTAND. DAD CAN BE GREAT SOMETIMES. IT'S JUST WHEN HE HAS A DRINK, HE GETS INTO THESE TERRIBLE MOODS.

▽ They talked for a while. Mr Swann came downstairs as Laura hung up.

YOU LIKE YOUNG TIM, DON'T YOU? ARE YOU HIS GIRLFRIEND? WHAT HAVE YOU TWO BEEN UP TO? AND THERE WAS I THINKING YOU WERE MY PRINCESS.

DAD, DON'T, YOU'RE EMBARRASSING ME. I'M TIRED, I'M GOING TO BED. GOODNIGHT.

A SHORT WHILE LATER...

PRINCESS, ARE YOU AWAKE? DADDY WANTS TO TALK TO YOU.

△ Laura stayed silent. She hoped her dad would think she was asleep. But he came into the room and closed the door.

MUM, I WISH YOU DIDN'T HAVE TO WORK SO LATE. CAN'T SOMEBODY ELSE DO A COUPLE OF SHIFTS?

▷ It was two weeks later. Mr Swann had been coming to Laura's room most nights when her mum was out at work.

▽ That night, Laura went to bed early, hoping her dad would not disturb her. But he woke her up a few hours later.

I DON'T KNOW WHAT'S THE MATTER WITH YOU LATELY LAURA. YOU KNOW I HAVE TO WORK.

YOU REMEMBER WHAT I SAID ABOUT THIS BEING OUR SECRET, DON'T YOU LAURA? YOU CAN NEVER TELL ANYBODY ABOUT IT.

YOU'RE VERY SPECIAL TO ME, PRINCESS. PEOPLE WOULDN'T UNDERSTAND. THEY'D TRY TO TAKE YOU AWAY FROM ME. YOU DON'T WANT THAT DO YOU?

I DON'T KNOW WHY THIS IS HAPPENING TO ME. IT DOESN'T FEEL RIGHT.

I KNOW, DAD.

YOU KNOW I DON'T DAD.

▷ After her dad had left, Laura lay awake for a long time. She felt frightened and confused.

Abusers use different methods to get people to go along with what is happening.

Abusers need to prevent anyone else from finding out about their behaviour because they know it is wrong. They will go to great lengths to make sure that the person they are abusing remains silent and keeps their 'special' secret. Some abusers will try to bribe a young person, promising gifts or special treats. Others use threats, making the young person believe that the abuse is his or her fault.

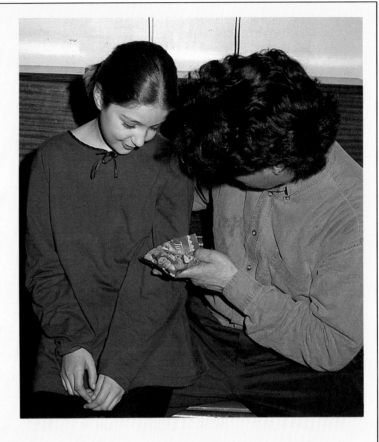

Sexual feelings are perfectly natural.

But it is important that any expression of these is appropriate. It is never acceptable for an adult to take advantage of a young person's curiosity about sex. A child should not feel that his or her own sexual curiosity is to blame for any sexual abuse by an adult.

Laura's dad has told her that what has happened is a secret.

We all have secrets. Revealing a secret someone has asked you to keep might seem like betraying that person. Abusers rely on this. They may frighten the abused person into believing that terrible things will happen if the secret is broken. They may even say that if the young person tells anyone, no one will believe him or her. In fact, this is very unlikely. Most adults will take allegations of abuse very seriously.

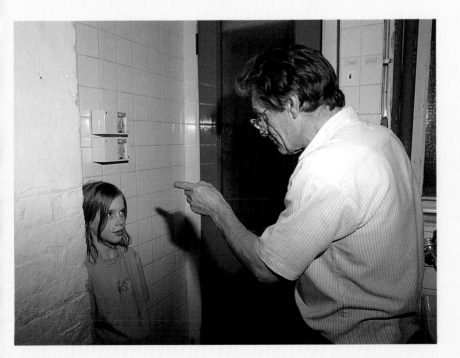

WHY DOES IT HAPPEN?

THERE IS NO SIMPLE REASON WHY CHILDREN ARE ABUSED OR WHY PEOPLE ABUSE THEM. CHILD ABUSE CAN HAPPEN TO GIRLS AND BOYS OF ALL AGES, FROM DIFFERENT RACES, RELIGIONS, CULTURES AND SOCIAL SITUATIONS.

The abuser is usually someone the young person knows and trusts – for instance a parent, another relative, a neighbour, a friend of the family, a babysitter, a carer or a teacher.
Drugs and alcohol can affect the way a person thinks and behaves. People may become more violent under their influence, and they have been a factor in some cases of abuse. Some people say that poverty and poor living conditions are contributory factors. Abuse of vulnerable young people may occur when the parent

or carer is unable to cope with his or her own feelings; he or she may take this unhappiness out on the children. Research has shown that people who were themselves abused as children are more likely to become abusers as adults.

Although most child abuse is carried out by someone known to the child, strangers may also abuse children. This is why it is important not to talk to or go off with strangers.

Money worries and poor housing can put a lot of pressure on parents and carers, especially if they do not have any support to help them cope. But much abuse also occurs in families where money is not a problem.

▽ It was two months later. One evening, after school, Tim saw Fatima being bullied by two other girls.

▽ The two girls let Fatima go. Fatima said they had been making fun of her.

Y, WHAT DO YOU THINK U'RE DOING? LEAVE HER LONE.

YOU STAY OUT OF THIS. IT'S NONE OF YOUR BUSINESS.

LOOK I'VE GOT TO GO. I DAREN'T BE LATE OR I'LL BE IN TROUBLE AGAIN. ARE YOU SURE YOU'RE OK, THOUGH?

SHE'S OUR FRIEND. THAT MAKES IT OUR BUSINESS.

NO HE'S NOT. WHAT DO YOU KNOW ABOUT IT ANYWAY? MY DAD'S OK. WHAT'S SO SPECIAL ABOUT YOUR PARENTS, ANYWAY?

YES I'M FINE. YOU GO - DON'T UPSET YOUR DAD AGAIN.

IT MUST BE AWFUL LIVING WITH YOUR DAD. HE'S ALWAYS SO ANGRY.

△ Tim was upset and ran off home.

MY DAD WOULD NEVER TREAT ME THE WAY HIS DOGS. HE'D NEVER DO ANYTHING TO HURT ME.

▽ When she had gone, Pat said she thought Laura had been acting strangely.

I'VE GOT TO BE GOING. I HAVE TO PICK UP LUKE TONIGHT. SEE YOU LATER.

I'VE NOTICED THAT TOO. SHE'S BEEN KIND OF DISTANT.

▽ At home, Laura made Luke his dinner, and waited for her mum to get home.

PLEASE LET MUM GET HOME BEFORE DAD DOES TONIGHT.

I THINK SHE'S FED UP ABOUT HER PARENTS WORKING ALL THE TIME. SHE ALWAYS ENDS UP HAVING TO LOOK AFTER HER LITTLE BROTHER. IT'S NOT FAIR.

Sometimes children become a 'go-between' for their parents. Parents may be so preoccupied with their negative feelings towards each other that they forget about the effects that the situation may be having on their children.

Sometimes, young people may abuse other children. Whoever abuses a child, and whatever his or her reason, it is never acceptable for this to happen.

Abusers can be male or female, young or old, and most look very ordinary. Because there is no one type of person who is more likely to abuse children than another, it can be difficult for others to know that a child is being abused. A child may not understand why those closest to her or him cannot see what is happening. He or she may feel let down because nobody has noticed what is going on. Even when a parent or carer is abusing a child, other members of the family may not be aware of it. People are usually shocked when abuse is discovered. Many find it hard to accept that abuse could be happening amongst people they know. They may mis-read signs which the child gives out. This is why it is important for anyone who is being abused to speak out about it.

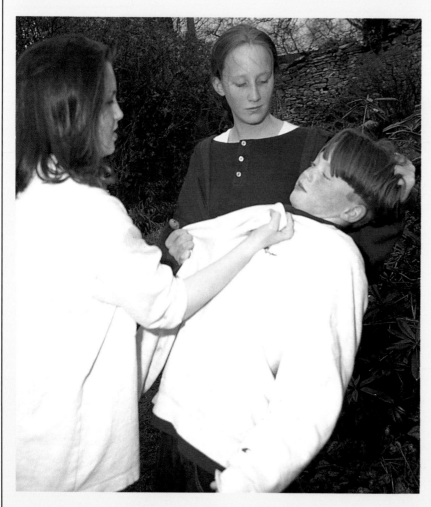

THE EFFECTS OF CHILD ABUSE

ABUSE CAN HAVE A DEVASTATING EFFECT ON PEOPLE'S LIVES, NOT JUST WHILE THEY ARE BEING ABUSED, BUT FOR YEARS AFTERWARDS.

The physical effects of abuse, unless an attack has been extremely violent, will usually disappear with time. The emotional turmoil can last much longer.

The effects of abuse will be different in each situation. Children may be confused about what is happening and why, particularly if someone they have loved and trusted seems suddenly to have turned against them. They may feel that nobody can be trusted. They might become more violent when they play. Children who are sexually abused often become obsessed about their bodies and may become sexually aggressive towards other children.

Although it is only the abuser who is at fault, many young people who are being abused feel guilty or 'dirty', as if they are doing something wrong. It is important that everyone is aware of how damaging child abuse can be, and learns to understand some of the ways in which young people might express their feelings. Children need to know that there are people they can talk to, and who will believe them.

Young people who are being abused may try to avoid other people as much as possible. They might not want to join in with their friends.

▽ A week later, Laura's teacher asked her to stay behind after class to discuss Laura's schoolwork.

△ Laura wanted so much to tell her teacher everything, but she felt too ashamed and confused.

▽ The following Monday was Fatima's birthday. Laura had been invited to her birthday party.

△ Laura was sorry. She apologised to Fatima, and went to dance with the others.

△ Laura had forgotten what it felt like to enjoy herself. Now she was having a really good time.

▷ Laura's good mood disappeared when the party finished. Her dad collected her.

Child abuse damages a person's feelings of self worth.

Abuse can make young people believe that they do not deserve to be loved. They may begin to hate themselves, and to feel that they should be punished, even though they have done nothing wrong. Children who have been abused may deliberately hurt themselves because they feel so desperate. Some have even tried to kill themselves because the feelings of despair can seem so overwhelming.

The effects of abuse are not always obvious.

People may hide the truth about their feelings for a long time. A young person may try to find other ways of coping with his or her feelings of confusion and anger.

Some young people develop strategies for coping with the abuse.

They might switch off from it, burying emotions which are too painful to face. Or they may even seem to invite the abuse sometimes, preferring that to the constant worry and fear about when, and if, it is going to happen.

Young people may become moody or withdrawn. They may lose interest in their appearance and their schoolwork. Or they may express themselves through violent pictures and aggressive behaviour. Sometimes, young people who are being abused will try to attract the attention of other adults by hurting themselves. They want somebody to notice that something is wrong, but are frightened of saying anything.

SHOULD I TELL?

YOU MIGHT THINK THAT IT WOULD BE EASY TO TELL SOMEBODY IF YOU WERE BEING HURT.

Unfortunately, this is not the case for most abused young people. Many are worried about what will happen if they tell. They believe that the consequences could be worse than the abuse itself.

You already know that abusers will go to great lengths to keep the abuse a secret. A parent or close relative who is abusing a young person may have said that telling will cause the family to break up. Children can still love the person who is abusing them, and may feel a sense of loyalty towards him or her. Or they might believe that they themselves will be blamed for causing the abuse in some way. An abused person may not know the right words to express what has been happening. Or he or she may not know who to turn to or might be afraid of not being believed.

People who suspect abuse is going on may also be unsure of what to do for the best. They may think "it's none of my business" or "I don't want to get involved". But nobody deserves to be abused. However difficult it may be to tell, abuse should not be allowed to continue. Every child deserves to be protected from abuse.

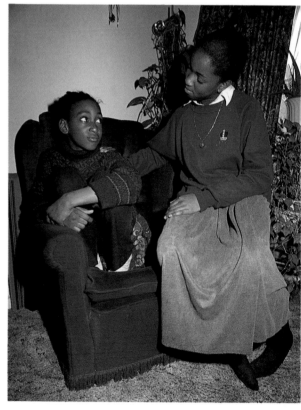

Being abused by someone trusted, can make it very difficult for young people to trust others. It can take a long time to build up the confidence to tell someone what has happened. But it is a brave and important step to take, and one which will help to stop the abuse.

▽ One morning, two months later, Stuart came to school with some news about Tim.

▽ Stuart explained he had overheard his parents talking. One of Tim's neighbours was a friend of his mother's.

THERE WAS A HUGE ARGUMENT AT HIS HOUSE OVER THE WEEKEND. THE NEIGHBOURS CALLED THE POLICE. THEY'VE ARRESTED TIM'S DAD.

WHY DID THEY ARREST HIS DAD?

APPARENTLY HE WAS REALLY DRUNK. HE'D HIT TIM'S MOTHER AND WAS THREATENING TIM.

THAT'S INCREDIBLE. HOW DO YOU KNOW ALL THIS?

WE WERE RIGHT THEN ABOUT HIS DAD HITTING HIM. WHERE'S TIM NOW?

NOBODY KNOWS. APPARENTLY HIS MUM'S TAKEN HIM AWAY FOR A WHILE. AT LEAST HE'LL BE SAFE NOW.

▽ It was two weeks to Christmas. Laura's sister Maggie had come home for the holdays.

I CAN'T WAIT TO FIND LAURA AND TELL HER. SHE'S BEEN SO WORRIED ABOUT TIM.

IT'S GOOD TO HAVE YOU HOME AGAIN. I'VE MISSED YOU, EVEN IF WE DID USED TO ARGUE ALL THE TIME.

I'VE MISSED YOU TOO. SO WHY DON'T YOU TELL ME EVERYTHING THAT'S BEEN HAPPENING WHILE I'VE BEEN AWAY?

▽ Laura wanted to tell Maggie about her own situation, but didn't know how. Instead, she talked about Tim.

▽ Laura said she was upset about Tim. A few days later, Laura, Luke and their mum got home to find Maggie and her dad arguing.

WHY WOULD HIS DAD HURT HIM LIKE THAT, DO YOU THINK? PARENTS AREN'T SUPPOSED TO HURT THEIR KIDS, ARE THEY?

WHAT ON EARTH IS GOING ON?

NOTHING TO WORRY ABOUT. JUST A LITTLE MISUNDERSTANDING. ISN'T THAT RIGHT MAGGIE?

NO, LAURA. SOME DO THOUGH, I'M AFRAID. YOU SEEM VERY QUIET. ARE YOU SURE YOU'RE ALRIGHT?

YOU COULD SAY THAT. SORRY MUM - I DIDN'T MEAN TO UPSET YOU.

▽ The next day, the two sisters went shopping. Maggie could tell Laura was unhappy.

WHAT MADE YOU THINK THAT, LAURA? I THINK WE NEED TO TALK. COME ON, LET'S GO IN HERE FOR A COFFEE.

WHAT WAS REALLY GOING ON LAST NIGHT? WERE YOU ARGUING ABOUT ME?

▽ They found a quiet table in the corner.

IS THERE SOMETHING YOU WANT TO TELL ME? YOU CAN TRUST ME, LAURA.

I DON'T KNOW WHO TO TRUST ANY MORE. I'M SO CONFUSED, MAGGIE.

▽ Eventually, Laura told Maggie that her father had been sexually abusing her.

PLEASE SAY YOU BELIEVE ME. I'M NOT MAKING IT UP, I SWEAR. YOU DON'T KNOW WHAT IT'S BEEN LIKE. I FEEL SO ASHAMED.

OF COURSE I BELIEVE YOU. AND I KNOW EXACTLY WHAT YOU'RE GOING THROUGH.

▷ Maggie told Laura that their dad had also abused her when she was younger.

ONE DAY HE STOPPED. HE SWORE TO ME HE'D NEVER DO ANYTHING LIKE THAT AGAIN. HE BEGGED ME NOT TO TELL ANYONE. HE SAID IF I DID IT WOULD BREAK UP THE FAMILY. NOW I FEEL RESPONSIBLE FOR WHAT'S HAPPENED. I SHOULD HAVE SAID SOMETHING.

DAD MADE ME PROMISE NOT TO SAY ANYTHING TOO. HE SAID IT WAS OUR LITTLE SECRET. HE MADE ME FEEL SPECIAL, BUT I FELT LIKE SUCH A BAD PERSON AT THE SAME TIME.

▽ When they arrived home, Laura asked what would happen now.

I TOLD DAD LAST NIGHT THAT IF I EVER FOUND OUT HE'D HARMED YOU OR LUKE, I WOULDN'T PROTECT HIM ANY MORE. DO YOU FEEL UP TO TALKING TO MUM?

YOU'RE NOT, LAURA. YOU'VE DONE NOTHING WRONG. NEITHER OF US HAS. DAD DOESN'T HAVE THE RIGHT TO DO THIS TO US.

△ Maggie told Laura this was what she and her dad had been arguing about. He had lied and said he hadn't touched Laura.

I THINK SO. I'M SCARED, MAGGIE.

22

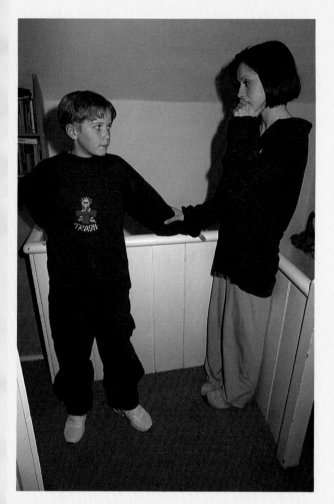

Maggie has discovered that her father has gone on to abuse her younger sister.
She has learned that a person who abuses one child may then do the same to a brother or sister in the same family. This can happen over a long period, without anyone being aware of what is going on, because the abused children have all been sworn to secrecy.

Laura is worried her mum won't believe her.
This fear can make it very difficult to speak out. Most people, however, know that a young person will not accuse someone of abuse unless there is a very good reason, and they will take the statement seriously.

Each abused person's experience will be different.
Some people may be more severely or frequently abused than others. No type of abuse, however, is ever acceptable.
  It is very unlikely that the abuse will 'go away'. Even if it does stop for one person, an abuser, like Laura's father, might eventually be tempted to abuse someone else. This is one reason why it is so important to tell someone you trust about what is happening.

CHILD PROTECTION AND THE LAW

CHILDHOOD IS A TIME WHEN WE LEARN TO MAKE SENSE OF THE WORLD AND WE DEVELOP A SENSE OF OUR OWN IDENTITY.

Child abuse interferes with this process. The laws of most countries recognise this and clearly state that child abuse is a crime. There are procedures laid down to ensure that children are protected.
These procedures will differ from place to place, but all put the welfare of the child first. When child abuse is suspected, the police and social services will become involved. They will talk to the child and to the person who is accused of the abuse. If the child is thought to be in danger, they may take her or him out of the home situation. This can be distressing for the child and the family, but they will not be kept apart longer than is necessary. There will also be other legal processes to be

faced. This might mean giving evidence in court. Although it may be frightening and upsetting to have to talk about what has happened, everyone will be making sure that the child suffers as little distress as possible. In some cases, children are allowed to record their evidence on video, so that they do not have to be questioned in court. Sometimes children may use dolls to help them show and explain what has happened to them, if they can't put it into words.

Allegations of child abuse are taken very seriously. Everything will be done to protect the child and to ensure his or her well-being.

▽ The girls spoke to their mum after their dad had left for work. Mrs Swann was devastated.

▷ Mrs Swann said she needed some time to think what to do. That afternoon, she called the police.

▽ When Mr Swann came home from work that evening, the police arrested him.

▽ The police took separate statements from Laura and Maggie.

▽ The next day, the social worker came to see Laura and Maggie at home. She explained what would happen next.

◁ Although she still felt guilty, Laura knew that what Maggie said was true.

It can be tempting to think that, once the abuse is discovered and stopped, life will immediately return to normal.

However, this is not the case. As the social worker has told Laura, there are still going to be hard times to face. Some children might be tempted to give up, but Laura understands why she must continue. She feels that nothing she has to go through will be worse than the abuse she has suffered.

Maggie and Laura's dad has denied the allegations of abuse.

Most abusers do not readily confess to their behaviour. Because the legal process gives everyone the chance to have a say, this may mean that the children will have to hear their abuser deny the allegations.

It is very difficult to listen to someone who you may still care about telling lies about you, and refusing to own up to what he or she has done. However, the courts will do everything they can to make the process as comfortable as possible for the child.

Abusers cannot be allowed to continue with their actions.

People have different ideas about what should happen to people who abuse young people. The decision usually depends on the individual case. Some abusers are sent to prison. Others may undergo therapy, where they are helped to think through what they have done and to change their behaviour.

FACING UP TO CHILD ABUSE

CHILD ABUSE IS A SUBJECT WHICH MANY PEOPLE DO NOT LIKE TO TALK ABOUT. MANY PEOPLE PREFER TO THINK THAT IT DOES NOT HAPPEN, OR THAT IT COULD NEVER AFFECT THEM OR ANYONE THEY KNOW.

Facing up to child abuse is not easy for anyone. But ignoring the problem will not make it go away.

The law recognises that child abuse is wrong. However, the legal process only begins when the abuse is discovered. The abuse has already happened; the child will already have suffered emotional or physical cruelty. Until we all confront the problem, children will continue to be abused.

It is important to believe a young person's statement, however incredible it may seem at the time. It is also vital to keep everything in perspective, so that any cases which might turn out not to be abuse are handled sensitively and quickly. In such instances, the child may need help and attention, to discover why he or she made the allegation in the first place.

Abusers may say that they know what they did was wrong, but they couldn't help it. In such cases they may also need help, to make sure that they never abuse anyone again.

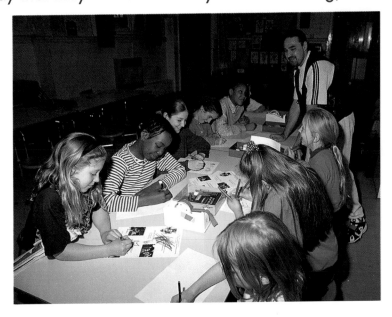

It is important to educate both children and adults, informing them about abuse and about the ways in which they can help to keep themselves safe.

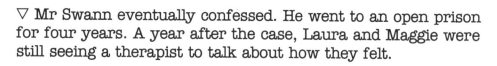

▽ Mr Swann eventually confessed. He went to an open prison for four years. A year after the case, Laura and Maggie were still seeing a therapist to talk about how they felt.

IT'S SO DIFFICULT TO TALK ABOUT, EVEN NOW. I KEPT IT INSIDE FOR SO LONG. PART OF ME LOVES HIM, BUT I HATE HIM FOR WHAT HE DID.

THAT'S NATURAL. IT'S VERY CONFUSING HAVING LOVING AND HATING FEELINGS LIKE THAT. THERE ARE SOME GOOD THINGS ABOUT YOUR DAD, BUT WHAT HE DID TO YOU WAS WRONG. WHAT ABOUT YOU, LAURA?

I STILL KEEP THINKING THAT LAURA WOULD HAVE BEEN ALL RIGHT IF I'D SAID SOMETHING SOONER.

YOU CAN'T THINK LIKE THAT, MAGGIE. IT'S NOT YOUR FAULT.

I DON'T KNOW IF I'LL EVER FEEL THE SAME WAY ABOUT HIM AGAIN. HE MADE ME FEEL SO GUILTY AND ASHAMED. I USED TO THINK I'D DONE SOMETHING TO MAKE IT HAPPEN.

MUM'S SEEN HIM, BUT I CAN'T YET. ACTUALLY, MUM'S BEEN TERRIFIC THROUGHOUT THIS WHOLE THING. SHE WAS THE ONE WHO HAD TO EXPLAIN EVERYTHING TO LUKE.

YOUR DAD'S IN A SPECIAL PROGRAMME NOW. THEY'RE TRYING TO HELP HIM. HE SAYS HE FEELS SORRY FOR WHAT HE DID, AND WANTS TO SEE YOU. HOW DO YOU FEEL ABOUT THAT?

▽ Laura's mum had moved house after the trial. Laura was at a new school. One evening, she bumped into Tim.

△ Both girls said it was still too soon for them.

IT'S GOOD TO SEE YOU. HOW ARE THINGS? I HEARD YOUR DAD'S MOVED BACK IN WITH YOU.

I KNOW. I THOUGHT SHE MIGHT BLAME ME FOR WHAT HAPPENED TO DAD, BUT SHE'S BEEN GREAT.

THAT'S RIGHT. HE'S STOPPED DRINKING. THINGS ARE MUCH BETTER AT HOME, NOW. EVERYBODY AT SCHOOL KEEPS ASKING HOW YOU ARE.

▽ In the end, Laura did decide to go to the party.

IT'S STUART'S BIRTHDAY IN A FORTNIGHT. HE'S HAVING A PARTY. WHY DON'T YOU COME ALONG?

MAYBE I WILL. I'D LIKE THAT.

YOU LOOK NICE, LAURA.

I'M GLAD TO SEE YOU LOOKING SO HAPPY. ARE YOU LOOKING FORWARD TO THE PARTY?

I'M A BIT NERVOUS, BUT IT WILL BE GOOD TO SEE MY OLD FRIENDS AGAIN.

Laura is not sure whether she will be able to forgive her dad.
In time, some people can forgive their abuser. Others may never feel able to do this. People who have been abused will never forget what has happened, but most are able to recover from the experience. This is not an easy process. It can take a very long time. People will need a great deal of help and support from others.

Tim's father is now receiving help to stop drinking.
He has admitted that he has a problem with alcohol, and that he becomes aggressive when he drinks. This is the first step in doing something about it. It may take a great deal of effort for an abuser to change his or her habits, but it can be done.

Every young person and child has rights.
It is up to everyone in society to ensure that children and young people are protected and that they are given the opportunity to develop physically and emotionally in a safe and positive way. Every young person has the right to enjoy life to the full.

WHAT CAN WE DO?

HAVING READ THIS BOOK, YOU WILL UNDERSTAND MORE ABOUT CHILD ABUSE AND THE WAYS IN WHICH IT CAN AFFECT PEOPLE'S LIVES.

You will know that no child or young person should have to put up with abuse, and that abuse is never the fault of the child.
If you suspect that abuse is happening, or know for certain that somebody is being abused, you should talk to somebody about it. Choosing the right person is important. Sometimes this might be a member of your family, a teacher or another older person whom you trust. If you yourself are being abused, remember that it can be stopped. The decision to tell can be a hard one, especially if you have strong feelings for the person who is abusing you, or if you have been sworn to secrecy or threatened. It may lead to some upheaval and may mean facing up to difficult feelings and situations. However, you have the right to be protected from abuse.

NSPCC (National Society for the Prevention of Cruelty to Children)
42 Curtain Road
London EC2A 3NH
Tel: 0800 800500 (24 hr helpline)
Website:
www.NSPCC.org.uk

The Children's Society
56-89 Margery Street
London WC1X OJL
Tel: 0207 837 4299
Website:
www.the-childrens-society.org.uk

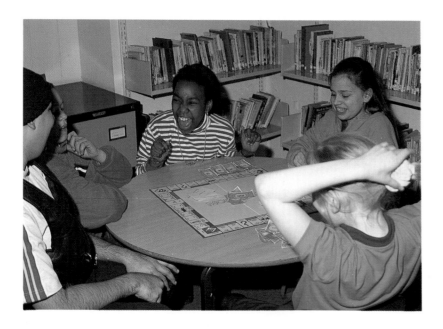

ADULTS ALSO HAVE A RESPONSIBILITY. THEY NEED TO LISTEN TO CHILDREN AND TO BELIEVE THEM, EVEN IF WHAT THEY ARE TOLD IS DIFFICULT TO ACCEPT.

Being more aware of the physical and emotional signs of abuse will also help.
Adults and young people who have read this book together may find it helpful to share their views about the issues raised. People who are experiencing abuse, or who would like more information, might like to talk to somebody who has experience of dealing with this kind of situation. The organisations listed below may be able to provide help and support.

Royal Scottish Society for Prevention of Cruelty to Children (RSSPCC)
41 Polwarth Terrace
Edinburgh EH11 1NU
Tel: 0131 337 8539
E-mail:
children1st@zetnet.co.uk

Childline
50 Studd Street
London
N1 0QW
Tel: 0207 239 1000
0800 1111 (24 hr helpline)
E-mail:
reception@childline.org.uk

The Samaritans
Head Office
10 The Grove
Slough SL1 1QP
Tel: 01753 216 5100
(information and enquiries)
See your phone directory
for the number of the local
24 hour helpline.
Website:
www.samaritans.org.uk

Survivors of Sexual Abuse
1-3 Hanworth Road
Feltham
TW13 5DT
Tel: 0208 890 4732

Child Abuse Prevention Society
PO Box 37-577
Parnell
Auckland
New Zealand
Tel: 00 649 638 8935

National Association for the Prevention of Child Abuse and Neglect Inc. (NAPCAN)
GPO Box 3658
Sydney
2001
Australia
Tel: 00 612 223 3565

INDEX

Photocredits
All the pictures in this book are by Roger Vlitos apart from pages: 1: Mal Bradley;
9 top, 23 bottom: NSPCC.
The publishers wish to acknowledge that all of the photographs in this book have
been posed by models.